LAND OF THE GIANT TORTOISE

Other books by Millicent Selsam published by Four Winds Press

---

How Kittens Grow
How Puppies Grow
All Kinds of Babies
Questions and Answers about Ants
Questions and Answers about Horses

LAND OF THE GIANT TORTOISE

THE STORY OF THE GALÁPAGOS

BY MILLICENT E. SELSAM

ILLUSTRATED WITH PHOTOGRAPHS BY LES LINE

Four Winds Press New York

LIBRARY OF CONGRESS CATALOGING IN PUBLICATION DATA
Selsam, Millicent Ellis.
Land of the giant tortoise.
SUMMARY: Describes two theories of the geological formation of the Galápagos Islands and explains the arrival and evolution of plant and animal life found there.
1. Natural history—Galápagos Islands—Juvenile literature. [1. National history—Galápagos Islands. 2. Galápagos Islands] I. Line, Les. II. Title.
QH198.G3S44 500.9′866′5 77–4897
ISBN 0–590–07416–4

Published by Four Winds Press
A Division of Scholastic Magazines, Inc., New York, N.Y.

Printed in the United States of America
Library of Congress Catalog Card Number: 77–4897
1 2 3 4 5 81 80 79 78 77

LAND OF THE GIANT TORTOISE

91°
PINTA (ABINGDON) ISLAND
Redonda Rock
Volcano Wolf
Volcano Ecuador
SANTIAGO (JAMES) ISLAND
Buccaneer Cove
Volcano Darwin
Albany Island
Point Espinosa
James Bay
Cowley Island
Rábida (Jervis) Island
Beagle Islands
Volcano Alcedo
Eden Island
FERNANDINA (NARBOROUGH) ISLAND
Elizabeth Bay
Pinzón (Duncan) Island
Sin Nombre Island
Volcano Sierra Negra
Crossman Islands
Volcano Cerro Azul
Santo Tomás
Puerto Villamil
Tortuga (Brattle) Island
ISABELA (ALBEMARLE) ISLAND
N
91°

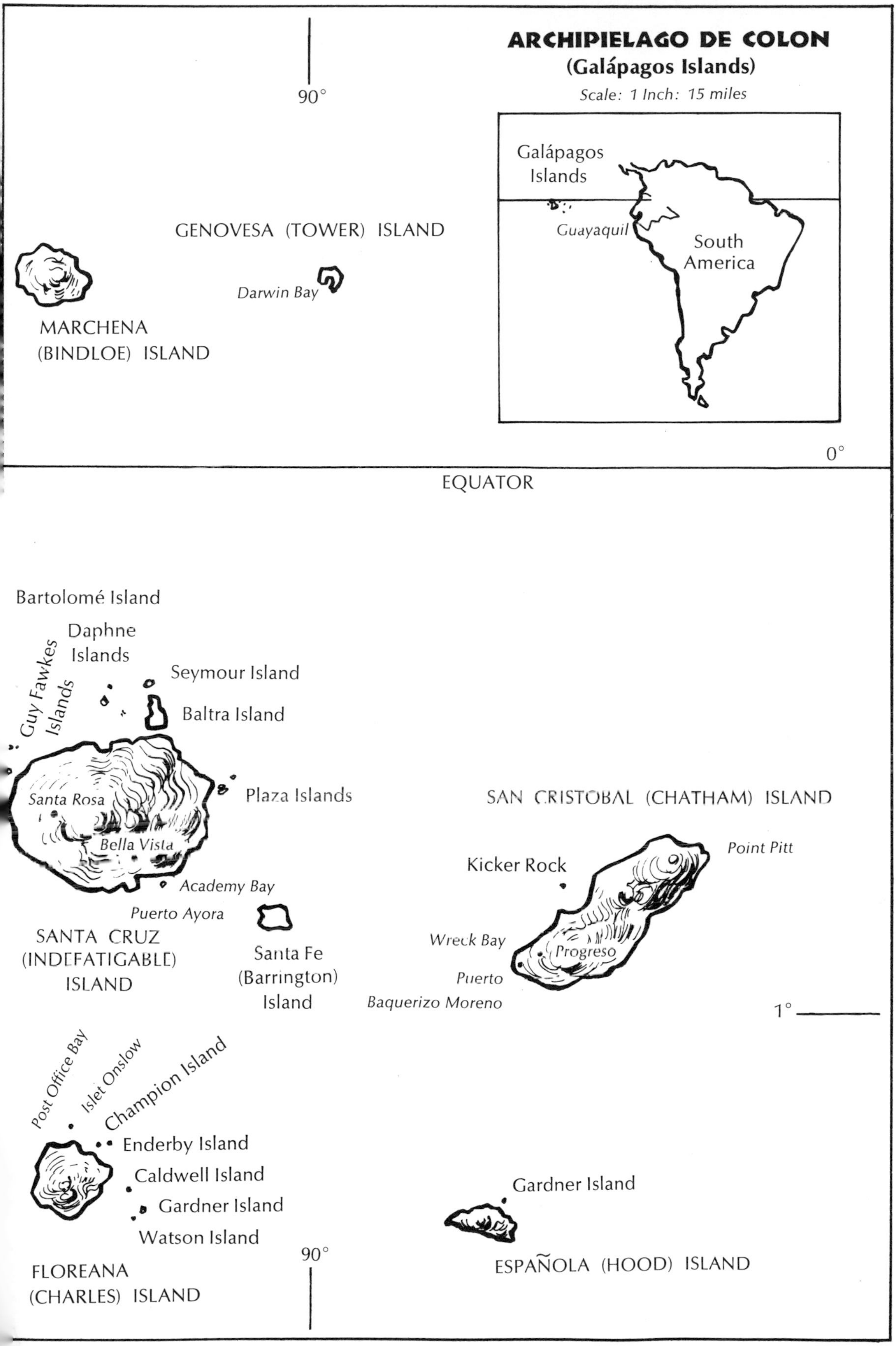

ARCHIPIELAGO DE COLON
(Galápagos Islands)
Scale: 1 Inch: 15 miles
90°
Galápagos Islands
Guayaquil
South America
GENOVESA (TOWER) ISLAND
Darwin Bay
MARCHENA (BINDLOE) ISLAND
0°
EQUATOR
Bartolomé Island
Daphne Islands
Guy Fawkes Islands
Seymour Island
Baltra Island
Plaza Islands
Santa Rosa
Bella Vista
Academy Bay
Puerto Ayora
SANTA CRUZ (INDEFATIGABLE) ISLAND
Santa Fe (Barrington) Island
SAN CRISTOBAL (CHATHAM) ISLAND
Kicker Rock
Point Pitt
Wreck Bay
Progreso
Puerto Baquerizo Moreno
1°
Post Office Bay
Islet Onslow
Champion Island
Enderby Island
Caldwell Island
Gardner Island
Watson Island
FLOREANA (CHARLES) ISLAND
90°
Gardner Island
ESPAÑOLA (HOOD) ISLAND

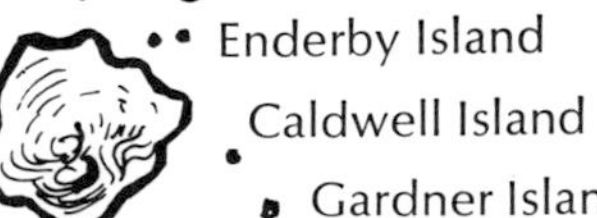

INTRODUCTION

There is a group of islands in the Pacific where a tortoise is so huge that a man can ride on its back . . . where there is the only seagoing lizard in the world that feeds on seaweed . . . where there is a penguin that breeds on the equator instead of on the cold lands near Antarctica . . . where there are prickly pear cacti as tall as trees . . . and where there is a cormorant bird that can't fly although everywhere else in the world cormorants do fly.

Where are these islands and how did these strange creatures get there?

Millions of years ago on the equator in the Pacific Ocean about 600 miles from South America, the earth began to move thousands of feet under the sea.

Big cracks opened in the sea floor. Boiling hot lava burst out of the cracks and in turn, made the water boil. Layer upon layer of lava steamed out of these submarine volcanoes and stiffened into rock. The rock piled up higher and higher, building mountains on the sea floor. Finally the undersea mountains reached the surface of the water. The volcanoes at the top of the mountains were still active. Lava kept pouring out of the tops of the volcanoes, and slowly but surely built up the islands we call the Galápagos Islands. The volcanoes did not all reach the top of the sea at the same time, so some islands are older than others in the group. There are now 15 large islands and about 40 smaller rocky islets. Lava is still pouring from the craters at the top of some of the islands.

DISCOVERY OF THE ISLANDS

For thousands of years no one knew about these islands way out in the Pacific Ocean. We still do not know for sure who the first men to see these islands were. Probably it was a king of the Inca Indians of western South America. An ancient Inca legend tells of King Tupac Yupanqui, the tenth Inca ruler, who in the middle of the fifteenth century,

is said to have sailed across the Pacific with a vast fleet of large sailing rafts to look for new lands to conquer. Perhaps he and his soldiers were the first human beings to have seen the Galápagos. But we do not know for sure.

However, there is proof that in 1535, the islands were discovered by Fray Tomás de Berlango, the Bishop of Panama. In March of that year, the bishop set sail on a small Spanish ship from a port in Panama. The ship was bound for Peru and was supposed to follow the coastline of South America. But when the ship reached the equator, the wind died down and a current started to carry it away from the coast. It drifted helplessly for eight days. Finally the crew sighted land, which turned out to be the Galápagos Islands. The bishop wrote a report to the King of Spain and told about these strange islands and the curious animals and plants he found on them. He was specially struck by the giant tortoises—huge turtles that lumbered over the rocky shores of the islands.

Several Spanish voyages were made to the islands after this and, in the seventeenth century, English pirates used the islands as a hideout and as a source of food. The giant tortoises were delicious and on board below deck these tortoises could be piled one on top of another and stay alive for a year.

dry zone

Piracy gradually slowed down, but in the eighteenth century British and American whalers started to make the Galápagos a stopping place for food and water. The waters around the islands were full of whales and the Galápagos tortoises provided fresh meat for the crews. Probably over two hundred thousand tortoises were taken from the islands through the years.

In any case, the islands became famous for the giant tortoises, and now bear the name Galápagos—the Spanish word for tortoise.

CHARLES DARWIN VISITS

Many British and American naval vessels also stopped at the islands. One of the British ships, the *Beagle*, sailed there in 1835. On board was a young naturalist, Charles Darwin. When he stepped ashore he was astonished to see the black volcanic rock, the scrubby dry-looking plants, the 30-feet high cactus trees! The fields of black lava swarmed with strange reptiles.

Black lizards that looked like small dragons were lying

sea lizards, also called marine iguanas

on the rocks. They had a crest of spines going down the back from head to tail. Their feet were webbed and they had tails flattened sideways. Darwin watched them jump into the water and move like crocodiles, their tails sweeping from side to side. They swam to where seaweeds were growing on the rocks or on the sea floor and chomped on them. Darwin was seeing the only sea lizards in the world.

Further inland, Darwin found land lizards, yellowish

orange beneath and a brownish-red color above. These lizards had round tails and toes without webs. They too had a row of spines running along their backs. They looked ferocious but they only fed on the cactus pads (spines and all) that fell to the ground. There were so many of their burrows everywhere that Darwin had trouble finding a spot where he could pitch his tent. This kind of lizard lived nowhere else on earth but on the Galápagos Islands.

Darwin was struck with wonder to see the giant tortoises. They looked like huge rocks taking a walk. Darwin watched their lumbering bodies move up paths through the undergrowth on their way to potholes of water in the mountains. There they drank their fill and lay around in the shade of trees or in the pools of water. They spent most of their time eating plants of all kinds—grasses, shrubs, and cactus pads—either those they could reach or those fallen to the ground.

Darwin noticed that there were tame mockingbirds on several of the islands he visited. They walked and ran and hopped. They chased flies, cracked open the shells of young crabs and snails, and the eggs of other birds. They were unusual because they were so tame and they had longer bills and shorter wings and tails than other mockingbirds.

The birds called finches seemed the most remarkable of all to Darwin. These birds, which looked like black spar-

PHOTO BY TUI DE ROY MOORE

giant tortoises

land lizard, also called land iguana

rows, were the most abundant land birds. Darwin took home to England a collection of finches. The collection showed that, within this one group of birds, there was a whole range of different kinds of beaks. Some had chunky beaks like heavy pliers. They could crack thick hard seeds. Some had long bills like long-nose pliers which they used to probe for insects. Some had bills like gripping pliers, good for eating fruits and buds. And in between there was a whole range of other shapes of beaks. There was even one woodpecker-type finch that could use a cactus spine or twig to pry insects out of bark.

Darwin wondered why one group of birds had so many different kinds of beaks. And why were there so few other land birds here? It looked as though one group of birds—the finches—had taken the place of the many different kinds of birds to be found on continents.

Charles Darwin visited the islands for only five weeks and he was astonished at the strange animals and plants he had seen. But just before he left, he discovered that the natives could look at any tortoise and tell from which island it came. When he heard this, he looked at his collection of mockingbirds and found that the same thing held true of them. The birds of one island were all of one kind and those from another island were of another kind, yet all were

mockingbird

PHOTO BY TUI DE ROY MOORE

cactus finch

tree finch

PHOTO BY TUI DE ROY MOORE

clearly related to one another. The same was true of the insects and plants he had collected.

Darwin knew that the Galápagos Islands were formed when undersea volcanoes exploded above the surface of the water. But he was puzzled about how the animals and plants got there. And why were there so many strange reptiles and birds found here and nowhere else on earth? Yet in spite of their strangeness, they resembled relatives in South America, Central America, and the Caribbean. As Darwin wrote, "It was most striking to be surrounded by new birds, new reptiles, new insects, new plants, and by innumerable trifling details of structure—to have the temperate plains of Patagonia, or the hot dry deserts of Northern Chile, vividly brought before my eyes."

Darwin didn't write about them, but he must have seen the sea lions everywhere in the waters around the islands. Female sea lions with their young could be found lying quietly on the rock shores. But usually a male sea lion was nearby patroling the area and watching over them to prevent other males from approaching. In the water the sea lions were sleek. They caught the waves and body surfed to shore. On land they moved clumsily.

baby sea lion

14

OTHER SCIENTIFIC EXPEDITIONS

After Darwin's visit, many other scientists made expeditions to the islands. They collected specimens from the different islands and saw many other strange and interesting plants and animals.

They saw the waved albatross, a large seabird with white head and neck and gray wavy lines running across its chest. This bird nests only on the Galápagos Islands and nowhere else in the world.

They saw a bird that can barely walk, can't fly and is a great swimmer and diver—the flightless cormorant. Its wings are stubby little things used to balance itself as it waddles to the sea.

They saw a strange gray gull with red rings around its eyes and pink feet. Its long pointed wings, like those of a swallow gave it its name—the swallow-tailed gull. At night its huge eyes help it to feed on the squid that rise to the surface of the sea.

They saw a peculiar little penguin—the Galápagos penguin—smaller and weaker than other penguins in the world.

They saw the short-eared Galápagos owl with its round yellow eyes.

Galápagos penguin

They saw the Galápagos hawk, a dark bird that sails over the islands and drops to the earth to pick up young birds and lizards.

They saw three kinds of large seabirds called boobies. The blue-footed booby had bright blue feet. The red-footed boobies had bright red feet. The masked booby had a black face mask around its orange eyes.

They saw scarlet crabs running over the black rocks.

They noticed something peculiar. There were hardly any mammals (those animals with fur or hair that bear young alive and feed them milk from special mammary glands). The only mammals they found were a few kinds of bats and some rats. Where, they wondered, were all the squirrels, bears, beavers, skunks, deer, raccoons, elephants, lions, tigers, that you see on the continents?

The insects on the islands were mostly ants, beetles, grasshoppers, a few butterflies and moths, and plenty of mosquitoes.

The scientists searched the pools and ponds of the islands but they could find no frogs, or toads, or salamanders.

They rediscovered what Darwin had noticed—that the animals and plants of each island were somewhat different from those on other islands. A different kind of giant tortoise lived on each of the islands. The mockingbirds were different looking on each island. And so on.

Why was this true? And how could the scientists explain why there were no frogs or other amphibians, and only a rat and a bat representing the many mammals of the world?

Perhaps all this could be explained if they could figure out how the animals and plants got to the islands in the first place.

PHOTO BY TUI DE ROY MOORE

blue-footed booby

red-footed booby

masked booby

The scientists came up with two different ideas. One group of scientists maintained that the Galápagos Islands must have been connected to Central or South America at one time. They pointed to two submarine ridges under the Pacific Ocean—one extending from Central America and another from South America. They said that these ridges might once have been above the sea and reached as far as the Galápagos Islands. Or, at least, they may have provided stepping stones to the islands. By short hops then, the plants and animals could have reached the islands.

But there is no real evidence yet that former islands beneath the sea served as stepping stones, or that the Galápagos actually were connected to the continent.

Most scientists today believe that the Galápagos Islands are truly oceanic, that is, they have never been connected to any continent since they rose in the sea. But they agree that they may have been closer or farther away from the South American continent at some time. Some of them think that the Galápagos Islands were once a large connected land mass which then sank, leaving only the tops of the volcanoes as the separate islands. Others say that each separate island came from a separate volcanic eruption.

Obviously, there is much we don't yet know. If the Galá-

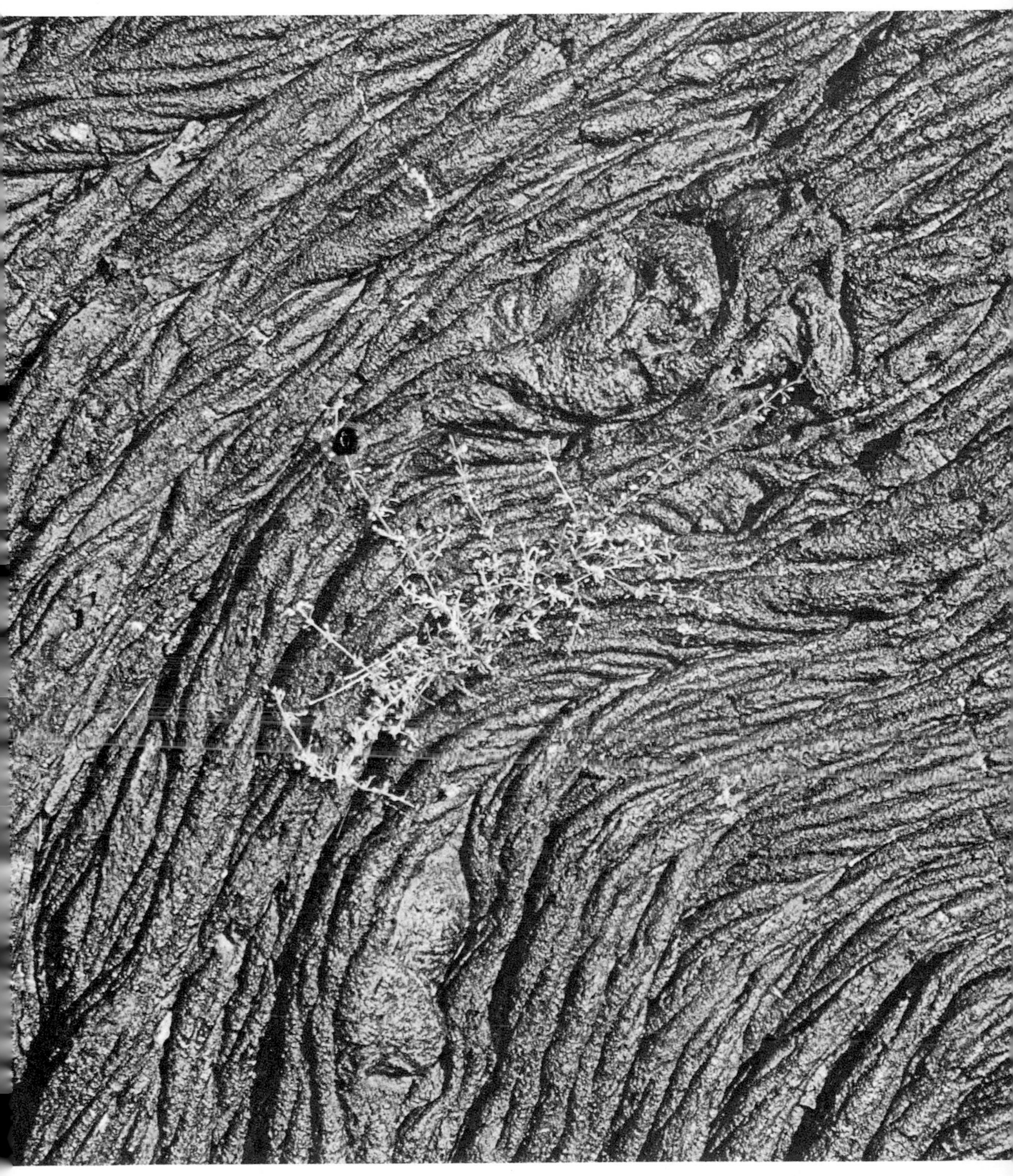

volcanic rock

pagos rose in the sea far from any land connection, how did the animals and plants get there? And what were the islands like when they did get there?

At first there was just hot lava. But the lava cooled and the sea and wind pounded the rock into soil along some of the shores. Up in the higher parts of the islands soil was formed when the hot sun and the cool rain caused the rock to split and gradually crumble into soil. Still, some of the rock remained tough and black, and plants could only grow in the cracks.

HOW THE PLANTS GOT THERE

Plants had to get to the islands first and prepare the way for the animals. The tortoise, for example, could not find food if the cactus and other green plants it feeds on were not there. Neither could the owl find food, for it fed on rats that depended on seeds for their food.

The plants probably came to the islands in many different ways.

swallow-tailed gull in flight

Seeds and fruits may have floated onto the shores. Many seeds have air pockets that act like life jackets and keep them floating on the surface.

The wind must have carried millions of seeds onto the islands. Some were light as dust—like the seeds of orchids. Others were members of the daisy family many of whose seeds have parachutes of silky hairs that keep them afloat in the wind. When the wind carrying the seeds reached the islands, the higher land on the slopes of the volcanoes stopped it, and forced it to drop its load of seeds.

Birds carried seeds to the islands in a number of different ways. Some birds brought seeds on their feet. Charles Darwin once removed some earth from the leg of a bird and placed it under glass. Eighty-two seedlings came up from that one bit of soil! Other birds carried many sticky fruits and seeds with hooks and barbs in their feathers. Birds also carry seeds in another way—they eat juicy fruits. The seeds pass through their digestive tract and are none the worse when they drop to the ground. Many of them then sprout and grow into fruit trees.

Gradually, over the years, the Galápagos Islands became covered with plants. But these plants are not like the ones that grow on lush tropical islands.

The Galápagos Islands are dry. It rains only about three months of the year. And so we find a dry zone of plants near

PHOTO BY HENRY M. MAYER

windblown seed of the dandelion

white "stick" trees

the shore. Only giant cactus, pale white "stick" trees with leafless branches, and other dry spiny and thorny plants grow there. Higher up, small trees begin to be mixed with the cactus. Still higher there is a moist shady zone, where clouds of moisture envelop the taller trees and larger bushes to be found there.

Many of the plants are peculiar. On some of the islands the prickly pear cactus has changed from a low-growing bushy plant to a tree 30 feet high with a thick reddish bark and heavy spines. Such prickly pear trees are found nowhere else in the world. On the larger and higher islands there are forests of "sunflower" trees. They are related to the sunflowers we know, but here on the islands they have become woody trees 40 to 50 feet tall.

HOW THE ANIMALS GOT THERE

When rivers in the jungles of South America flood their bank, great chunks of trees, bushes, and vines fall into the water and are carried down toward the sea. Tangled

masses of this vegetation jam together into rafts and when they reach the sea, they are carried by sea currents.

There is a cold river of water in the Pacific Ocean that starts from the Antarctic and flows along the coast of South America. At the equator it turns off toward the Galápagos Islands. It is called the Humboldt Current. There is another warm current that flows toward the islands. It comes from Panama. Both of these currents can easily carry the rafts of vegetation to the islands. Natural rafts like these have been seen hundreds of miles off the coast of South America and one scientist actually timed the movement of one of them. It drifted toward the Galápagos at the rate of 75 miles in a day! Another scientist reported seeing a raft of vegetation over a block long floating on the sea. On it there were trees over 30 feet tall.

Many animals and plants could have arrived at the Galápagos on such rafts. Lizards, turtles, and snakes have tough scaly skins. They could float on such rafts and survive even a journey of hundreds of miles. So could snails hidden inside their shells. So could tough-skinned beetles. But if frogs or salamanders were on such a raft, the salt water would probably injure them and they would not make a successful landing at the islands. This would explain why there are no frogs or salamanders on the Galápagos Islands.

Mice or rats could have floated on such rafts because

short-eared Galápagos owl

they are small. But other larger mammals would not be able to survive a 600-mile journey on the sea. That is why there are no native mammals but rats and bats that probably flew over on their wings.

Today there are other mammals on the islands but they were brought there by pirate ships and whalers and all the other kinds of ships that have stopped at the islands. They left off the dogs, cats, goats, and cattle that now run wild over many of the islands of the Galápagos.

Many insects probably were carried to the islands hidden away in cracks and holes of the trees and bushes on the rafts that floated there. They were the kinds that can bore into dead branches and twigs or dig into the soil around the plants.

Other insects came by air. They, like the seeds, may have hitchhiked on the feathers or feet of birds. Even a floating feather can be covered with insect eggs!

Insects can also drift in high air currents. Special nets on airplanes have caught hundreds of different kinds of insects thousands of feet up in the air. Many must have landed on the islands.

Some butterflies and moths might have reached the islands on their own wing power. Or, if they are the kind that migrate, they could have been blown off course and landed on the Galápagos that way.

Birds could have come to the Galápagos on their own wings. Many seabirds are strong fliers and can easily cross long distances over the water. The Galápagos albatross and the swallow-tailed gull probably came this way. The flightless cormorant may have come when its wings were large and strong and later lost its ability to fly.

Even weak-winged birds that were migrating over sea routes may have been carried to the islands by strong winds. Owls have landed on ships hundreds of miles from shore. So have many other small birds. The first finches and mockingbirds that landed on the Galápagos most probably came this way.

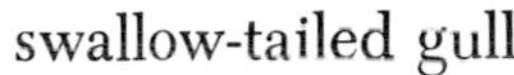

swallow-tailed gull

The Galápagos penguin must surely have come to the islands via the Humboldt Current that swept it from the tip of South America. This penguin looks very much like the penguin that lives around the Strait of Magellan.

The hardest question of all to answer is how the huge Galápagos tortoises got to the islands. Many scientists have puzzled over how they could have crossed 600 miles of open ocean. We do know now that tortoises can float on the sea for a few days and can go for very long periods of time without food and water. Perhaps only their eggs, or small young ones came on rafts of vegetation.

Millions of years ago very large tortoises lived on the continents of North and South America, Europe, and Asia. They gradually disappeared, probably because mammals like deer, lions, tigers, wolves, and dogs ate their eggs and young. But hundreds of thousands of years ago, some of these tortoises managed to get to the Galápagos Islands. There, without mammals to destroy them, they gorged on the plants, survived, and increased in numbers.

Another puzzling question is how the tortoises got to all the islands of the Galápagos. They don't seem to go from one island to another at all now. But if, as some scientists say, the Galápagos were once one large mass of land with many volcanoes, there is a possible explanation. The tortoises could have arrived at the land mass long ago. Then

albatross

scarlet crabs

the land could have sunk so that the tops of the volcanoes became different islands. In that way the tortoises could have become separated on the different islands and changed so that each type became a little different from the ones on the neighboring islands. This is a logical theory, but up to now there is no proof that this actually happened.

Whatever way the animals and plants reached the Galápagos, it was a slow process, and may have taken thousands of years. Now on the Galápagos Islands we have strange animals and plants that live nowhere else in the world.

How did this happen? And why are there such differences between the animals and plants on each island?

HOW THE ANIMALS AND PLANTS OF THE GALÁPAGOS CAME TO LOOK AS THEY DO

We know that tortoises arrived at the Galápagos Islands hundreds of thousands of years ago. Perhaps at that time, the adults were not as big as they are now. Or perhaps the first settlers were very young tortoises. Either way they

PHOTO BY TUI DE ROY MOORE

could have floated on rafts. At any rate, they crossed the ocean and reached the Galápagos.

The mystery is how they got to look different from each other on the different islands. All over the earth during the hundreds of thousands of years since the tortoises arrived, animals and plants have been changing, just as they changed all through the past history of life on earth. The tortoises on the islands changed, too. Let us see how.

Suppose a female with eggs ready to be laid landed on one of the islands. She had a dome-shaped shell and a short neck and short legs. When the eggs hatched, suddenly there was a small group of tortoises on the island. They found lush vegetation in the hills. The young tortoises fed on the juicy plants and multiplied. In time there were thousands of dome-shaped tortoises with short necks and legs on this island.

Now suppose another female ready to lay eggs landed on another island of the Galápagos. But this island had nothing growing on it but cactus and spiny bushes. The eggs hatched and the tortoises fed on the sparse vegetation.

saddleback tortoise

PHOTO BY TUI DE ROY MOORE

PHOTO BY TUI DE ROY MOORE

tortoise with dome-shaped shell

After a while, there were lots of tortoises but much of the vegetation was used up. Now those tortoises that happened to have longer necks and legs than the others could reach up and get the juicy pads of cactus that grew higher up on the plant. If some of them had shells raised high around the neck like a saddle, they could also stretch their necks higher. These tortoises would grow up and lay more eggs than the ones that did not get enough food.

In time, the tortoises that could not reach such food would die out. And gradually, over the years, more and more of the tortoises on this island would come to have longer necks, longer legs, and "saddleback" shells. They would look very different from the tortoises with dome-shaped shells and short legs and necks that lived on the other island.

The changes came about because the tortoises lived on separate islands where the conditions were different. On each island tortoises best suited to the conditions there survived, mated with each other, and laid more eggs than others. Gradually a new kind of giant tortoise came to be. Fifteen distinct kinds of tortoises developed on the Galápagos Islands, 11 of which survive today.

The evolution of tortoises and prickly pear cactus on the Galápagos Islands seems to have gone along together.

On some islands of the Galápagos, the prickly pear cac-

tus is a low-growing plant with soft spines. On others, it is tall as a tree, with a thick bark and sharp spines. How did this happen? A good guess would be that on islands where there were never any tortoises, the cactus would be bushy and low growing while on the islands where there are tortoises, the cactus would probably be treelike. This "guess" is actually true. On islands with tortoises the low-growing types of prickly pear cactus were destroyed while those cacti that were taller and had sharper spines escaped being eaten and were able to grow up and produce seeds. Eventually these cacti became tall as trees.

How can we explain the flightless cormorant? Everywhere else in the world cormorants have wings and fly, but on the Galápagos their wings are short and stubby and they cannot fly. Probably cormorants came to the Galápagos long ago when they still had wings. Perhaps cormorants with shorter wings than usual hatched out of the eggs that were laid on the islands. They dived for fish as all cormorants do and were able to survive and increase in number. Cormorants with longer wings probably flew off, but these short-winged ones had to stay. If this happened on the continent, these birds that could not fly would not last long because they would be killed by the mammals that lived there, too. But here on the Galápagos Islands, the short-winged ones could live, grow up, mate, and lay more eggs.

tree cactus

In the course of time this rare kind of cormorant would be found living on the Galápagos Islands and nowhere else in the world.

How can we explain the finches with their many different kinds of bills? On continents, finches are birds with short thick bills good for cracking seeds. But on the Galápagos there are finches that feed on many different kinds of food, and have different sizes and shapes of bills.

Long, long ago, finches arrived on the Galápagos. There were very few other birds on these islands so the finches could spread out and try the many different kinds of food available. Some of them may have had bills a little pointier than the others and could dig insects out of wood. They would stay where they found these insects and, separated from other finches with thicker beaks, they would mate with each other. In each generation, those with pointier bills that could probe insects out of tree trunks and branches more efficiently would grow up and lay more eggs than others. Over the course of thousands of years, a finch with a pointed bill would develop.

On another island, or even in another place on the same island, the thick-billed finches might find heavy seeds they could crack better than the others. They would stay where this food was found and, separated from other finches, would mate with each other. In each generation the thicker-

flightless cormorant

PHOTO BY MILLICENT E. SELSAM

billed finches that were suited to the heavy type of seeds would grow up faster and lay more eggs than the others. Over thousands of years, a very heavy-billed finch would develop.

The finches shared a common ancestor that long ago came to the islands, but in time the finches began to develop different bills as they took advantage of the many

different places on the islands where they found different kinds of food, and where there were few other birds to compete with.

If these birds got separated on different islands of the Galápagos and could not mix with others at all, they might have become different *species.* (A species is a kind of plant or animal that usually cannot mate or cross with individuals of another kind.)

There are now 13 species of finches on the Galápagos. Six species feed mostly on the ground, eating seeds of dif-

large ground finch

PHOTO BY TUI DE ROY MOORE

ferent sizes and hardness. Each of the six species has a bill suited to a certain kind of seed. Three kinds of tree finches excavate insects from the wood of trees. One finch feeds on the insects it finds on leaves. One kind feeds on buds and flowers, and two woodpecker types use twigs or spines to dig insects out of holes in trees.

These finches have taken the place of the warblers, woodpeckers, robins, tanagers, blackbirds, and orioles that live on the continents.

THE FUTURE

Until this century nothing was done to preserve the unique plants and animals of the Galápagos Islands. Pirates, whaling boats, naval ships, and merchantmen left their mark because they took hundreds of thousands of giant tortoises from the islands. Unfortunately, these tortoises provided the only fresh meat available for hundreds of miles.

Even at the time of Darwin's visit, tortoises were already

beginning to disappear from a few of the islands. By the 1930s, there were only about nine to ten thousand tortoises left out of the hundreds of thousands that lived there before man came to the islands.

There were only small settlements on the islands but the people in these settlements hunted and killed thousands of tortoises for their thick layer of fat under the shell.

Also, the ships that stopped at the islands and the people who settled there brought cattle, donkeys, goats, pigs, dogs, rats, and cats. They ran wild and destroyed animals and plants.

The goats destroyed the vegetation. They ate up every plant that grows and even chomped through the thick trunks of the cactus trees till the tops fell over and they could eat the spiny pads. In this way, much of the food supply of the tortoises and land iguanas was destroyed.

The pigs and dogs ate the eggs and young of the giant tortoises, land iguanas, and birds.

Cats attacked the birds and young iguanas.

Rats ate the eggs of the tortoises, iguanas, and birds.

Finally in 1935 there was a hundred-year celebration of Charles Darwin's visit. At this time the government of Ecuador issued laws to protect the animals and to set aside certain Galápagos Islands as reserves.

Nothing much was done to see that the protective laws

were carried out until 1959, when scientists all over the world decided that international help was needed. An organization called the Charles Darwin Foundation was set up to protect and study the unusual plants and animals of the Galápagos.

A research station was set up on the island of Santa Cruz where scientists of every nationality could come to study. As a result of their work, we have today a list of practically every plant and animal that lives on each island of the Galápagos.

At the same time, the government of Ecuador declared all the uninhabited areas of the Galápagos a national park to be controlled by the National Park Service of Ecuador. The animals and plants are now protected by strict laws.

No animals or plants of the protected areas are allowed to be taken from the islands. At the Darwin station, they collect tortoise eggs and protect them while they hatch and grow to a size too big to be swallowed by dogs and pigs.

There are now four settlements on the islands and the people in them have been taught about the unique value of the native plants and animals.

Tourists are being encouraged to visit the islands. But the station controls the places they are allowed to go. For example, they are not allowed into nesting areas where

PHOTO BY MILLICENT E. SELSAM

they might disturb the birds. Littering is forbidden and nothing may be taken from the islands.

There is still danger from the fact that tourists may accidentally bring bacteria or viruses or plants that could upset the natural life of the islands.

For instance, mosquitoes were accidentally introduced to Hawaii where there had never been any before. The mosquitoes carried a virus that killed a great number of the native honeycreeper birds. Nobody could have predicted this and that is why the Galápagos Islands need an effective plant and animal quarantine to preserve them as they are. New pests or germs accidentally introduced can destroy rare species.

The Galápagos are definitely worth preserving, for they have the most unique collection of animals and plants that can be found anywhere in the world.

Only on these islands are there prickly pears as tall as trees.

Only on these islands is there a seagoing lizard that feeds on seaweed.

Only on these islands is there a penguin that breeds on the equator instead of on the cold lands near Antarctica.

Only on these islands is there a cormorant that can't fly.

Only on these islands is there a gull that flies and feeds at night.

PHOTO BY TUI DE ROY MOORE

seabirds

marine iguana and swallow-tailed gull

bull sea lion

Only on these islands is there a tortoise so huge that a man can ride on its back.

And only on these islands are there finches with all manner and shapes of beaks that seem to have taken the place of the many different kinds of birds that make up the bird world on the continents.

Charles Darwin, the young naturalist who stopped at

the Galápagos Islands in 1835, later became a world-famous scientist. For years after he visited the Galápagos, he puzzled over the strange animals and plants he found there. He became convinced that life had arrived on the islands from the continents nearby and then had changed or "evolved" in an entirely different way from the animals and plants on those continents. This was striking evidence for his theory of evolution, which he wrote in 1859, 24 years after he saw the Galápagos Islands. The book that describes his theory is called *The Origin of Species,* and changed the history of biology.

INDEX